Homeless to Doctor of Nursing Practice: One Nurse's Journey

A Memoir

Dr. Cora S. King, FNP-BC

This book is dedicated to my mother, Ronda Jean, my best friend and forever champion. I love you, old girl.

To my daughter, Phoenix Raeign, my first love, thank you for being born. Mommy loves you.

To my grandson, Major, my little broke best friend, a true gentleman and old soul who keeps Granny in the fight. Granny loves you beyond measure.

To my father Harold Sr., who stepped in to serve as a father figure and mentor to Major and who has served in that role since his birth and continues to do so; you have my forever gratitude. I love you, Pops.

To my stepfather, Ronald William, thank you for helping my mother to raise and provide me, my older sister, and younger brother with a great life. I love you, Ron.

To my friend Tina W-M, a.k.a. Tina Teenz, who I always give credit to for being that person who set me back on course when I fell off. I love you, friend.

To the rest of my family and friends who stuck by me no matter what, through thick and thin on this journey, this marathon, I love you all to pieces and am grateful for you.

Lastly,

To all the aspiring and current nurses, to everyone in the healthcare profession, to those needing inspiration across the globe, I SEE YOU! STAND UP!

We are only going up from here, GOD BLESS EVERYONE!

Rest In Heaven Cordell, Denise, Grandma Eloise, and Vanessa

EVERYONE HAS THE GOD-GIVEN RIGHT TO
SHARE THEIR TESTIMONY IN THE HOPES
THAT THEY MAY INSPIRE OTHERS,
RESULTING IN A POSITIVE IMPACT ON THE
WORLD IN WHICH THEY LIVE.

FOREWORD

The mission is inspiration. The goal is transparency. This book is for those who need inspiration to do whatever it is you want to do. It doesn't have to be nursing. Just recognize that whatever it is you want to do, you can do it. With faith and trust in your Higher Power, you can do whatever it is you set your heart and mind to. YOU CAN DO IT!

TABLE OF CONTENTS

FOREWORD v

Part 1: Before the Storm viii

    CHAPTER 1 1

    CHAPTER 2 6

Part 2: Homeless 14

    CHAPTER 3 15

    CHAPTER 4 18

    CHAPTER 5 21

    CHAPTER 6 25

    CHAPTER 7 29

    CHAPTER 8 33

Part 3: Journey to Nursing 40

    CHAPTER 9 41

Part 4: Becoming an LPN 46

    CHAPTER 10 47

    CHAPTER 11 53

Part 5: Becoming an RN 58

    CHAPTER 12 59

    CHAPTER 13 62

    CHAPTER 14 67

Part 6: Becoming an FNP 72

    CHAPTER 15 73

    CHAPTER 16 75

    CHAPTER 17 78

    CHAPTER 18 81

Part 7: If I Can Do It, So Can You! 88

    CHAPTER 19 89

PART 1: BEFORE THE STORM

CHAPTER 1

"Cora, wake up! I think I need to call the ambulance!" said Zora.

"What?"

"I feel sick, I think I have to call the ambulance!"

"Girl, go to the bathroom. All that smoking weed and drinking you were doing earlier...you know you don't normally do that. You're just feeling sick, go to the bathroom."

"No for real, I think I need to call the ambulance," said Zora.

"No! Just go to the bathroom, then get some water and go to bed. You'll be okay," I said as I sat up. "Go."

I glanced over at my daughter, Phoenix, who was fast asleep as the light from underneath the bathroom door gently illuminated her. It was August of 2003; she was a little over two months old and was snugly tucked in next to me.

I love her so much; I thought as I waited for Zora to finish up in the bathroom. After coming out, she got some water from the kitchen and lay back down on her pallet at the foot of my bed. I peeked over the edge to make sure she was okay. She had fallen back to sleep. I returned to the top of the bed next to Phoenix, pulled the covers over me and drifted off to sleep. The next time I would open my eyes, the EMS and the Greensboro Police Department would be standing in my apartment.

The noise of voices chattering, and police radios blaring had awakened me. It seemed to be coming from my living room which was on the other side of my bedroom door. I opened the door and walked in as EMS was examining Zora as she sat on a stretcher. I was in utter disbelief at all the EMS and police officers standing in my apartment. Zora had phoned EMS after all.

As I looked around, one officer said, "Do we have permission to search your apartment?" I thought about Phoenix who was still sleeping quietly in my bedroom. I didn't want to further aggravate the situation because of this, so I hesitated before reluctantly saying, "Go ahead." I was ignorant of my right to refuse the request without a warrant.

The commencement of search was immediate. I always kept my apartment clean and immaculate, so to see it being rummaged through by foreign hands upset me. "You aren't going to find shit," I mumbled under my breath. Mild paranoia set in as my mind shifted back to Phoenix. *I need to get my baby out of here; she doesn't need to be around this shit! Why did Zora have to call the EMS and police to my apartment! How am I going to get Phoenix out of here?*

I went back into my bedroom and called Tonya for help. She was Zora's and my sorority sister. She was also Zora's line sister. When she picked up the phone, I began to explain what Zora had done and what was currently happening. I told her that I was terrified that my baby would be taken. I asked her if she could please come to the apartment and act like Phoenix was her baby. I would say that I was babysitting for her so that she could take Phoenix with her. She agreed to come over. We hung up the phone and I walked back into the living room.

Tonya arrived at my apartment moments later with another good friend of ours, Tookie. I opened the door with a look of desperation on my face and gave several nonverbal hints to Tonya to take Phoenix and go, but she didn't. Instead, she and Tookie sat at my dining room table quietly observing. Meanwhile I was quietly melting on the inside. My naiveté had me thinking, *Lord, I'm going to jail, and they're going to take my baby! She's innocent. She was just born AND she's asleep. HELP ME JESUS!*

While some officers continued to search the kitchen and living room, a couple of police officers made their way into my bedroom. I quickly followed.

Upon entering, one police officer looked at the bed and curiously asked, "Who's baby is that?"

"Mine," I said quick as lightning with a "have you lost your damn mind" look on my face. If Tonya wasn't going to take her for some unknown reason, I damn sure wasn't about to deny her. I'd just have to stand on it.

"Okay," said the officer.

I watched intently, with my head on the swivel, as they rummaged through my entire room and closet.

My heart dropped when I heard one officer say, "We got something!"

Got what? I thought to myself, there isn't shit in here!

He then spun around like he was Indiana Jones who just discovered the Holy Grail. "Right here," he said.

"Right here where?" I said to myself. As I looked at the white box he was holding, I thought, *well damn.* I had forgotten all about that fifty count Dutch Master box with razor blades, empty clear baggies, seeds, and stems in it. I hadn't smoked since I got pregnant with Phoenix! Now I was really shaking in my boots.

Lord, I'm going to jail, and they're going to take my baby! I thought.

The officer then belted out, "We're charging you with misdemeanor possession of marijuana and drug paraphernalia."

What? All of that for an empty box? I knew what a misdemeanor was, and I thought paraphernalia or "nalia" were specific clothes and accessories.

"What's paraphernalia?" I asked.

"It's the box, razor blades, and empty baggies. The seeds and stems are less than half of an ounce. That's why you're being charged with a misdemeanor and not felony possession," the officer responded.

"Oh." I looked sadly over at my baby, feeling like I had failed her.

The officer took notice. "No, you're not going to jail, but we are going to write you a citation and it will have a court date on it. You will have to show up or you'll have more problems."

"Yes sir," I said without hesitation. Then, out of nowhere, just like that, as quick as they came, they were gone. Everyone. One minute was chaos, the next minute was silence. I was just grateful that Phoenix was okay. I sat on the bed and looked over at my baby who remained asleep throughout the whole ordeal. I thanked God that she was safe and not taken from me.

Why did I have this back to college party shit at my apartment anyway? I had already graduated from UNCG. Where was Zora?

I received a call the next day. "I'm okay sis," said Zora, "they released me."

"No shit, Sherlock. I told you that you were going to be okay."

In my heart though, I was dead ass glad she was okay. I would be lying if I were to say I hadn't been worried about her. I mean, she felt the need to call the ambulance after all. If you feel sick enough to call EMS, you must really feel bad. At the end of the day, I couldn't be mad at that. I just knew I wouldn't be having any other gatherings at my apartment. Little did I know, the apartment complex managers shared the same sentiment. I found that out one day when I arrived at the leasing office to pay my rent for the upcoming month.

CHAPTER 2

I stepped into the leasing office with Phoenix in my arms and handed over my money order for the rent. The leasing agent gladly accepted it and then stated, "We are not renewing your lease at the end of your contract. There have been too many disturbances at your residence."

"What?" I blurted out. I pleaded with the leasing agent, explaining to her that I just had a baby, and I didn't have anywhere else to go and that I always paid my rent on time.

"I'm sorry," she said.

"What can I do?" I asked.

"There's nothing you can do, Miss King. Again, I'm sorry."

I thought to myself there had been two previous "disturbances" at my residence before, but the last one truly wasn't my fault. In order to explain, I must backtrack to bring you up to speed.

I "met" my daughter's father, Luke, before I met him in real life. Before I knew who he really was. How is that possible, you might ask? When I graduated from the University of North Carolina at Greensboro (UNCG) in 2001, Zora, Tonya and I lived together for a brief period before Tonya and I moved out and got our own apartments. We had a neighbor who lived above us who would come down to the apartment and chill with us on occasion. He was a good guy, and we always enjoyed his company.

I was sitting at home in my apartment one day when I received a phone call from Zora. "Do you remember our neighbor from Alamance Church Road, Angel?"

"Yes," I said.

"Well, he was murdered last night."

My mouth dropped open. "What?"

She began to explain how he was shot and killed, and how the police were actively looking for the people responsible.

"Well, who was it?" I asked.

"I don't know," she said. "I was told that one of the guys they're looking for is a guy who is really tall who was seen running up the street shortly after it happened."

A really tall guy? I thought. "Well, he isn't going to be able to get far like that, sis," I said.

After our conversation, all I could think about was that Angel had children and a devoted girlfriend. My heart was broken. How does a woman deal with that kind of pain? How does she have the strength to go on? I thought about how there were children who will never see their father's face again. I thought about how unfair life can be. I thought about how he didn't deserve that. No one does.

About a week later, while I was working as a bartender at one of the hottest spots in Greensboro at that time, L's Sports Bar and Lounge, the most beautiful guy that I had ever seen walked in. He was a tall drink of water as the old folks would say. Fine with a capital F. He was wearing a red baseball cap, a white T-shirt and a pair of tan Dickie shorts that hung past his knees. I don't remember the shoes he had on because I never paid attention to them and couldn't see them from behind the bar anyway.

My immediate thought was, *I want him.* Lord knows I had no idea what I was asking for, let alone what I was in for. My boss, L, had come behind the bar to put up some bottles and saw me gazing at him.

"Oh, that's Luke," he said.

"Well, he's fine. I want him."

He laughed. "I have known him since he was young. I helped raise him up in these streets. If you want him, why don't you talk to him?"

"No way!" I said. I was shy. Really shy. What would he want with me anyway? His ass was fine. I know he had all the women he desired. "No," I reiterated, "and you better not tell him either."

"Okay," L said and walked away.

While L and I had been speaking, I noticed that Luke had walked through the club and out to the back patio. The patio area had a dirt floor with three picnic style benches and a table that was set up with chips, condiments, Styrofoam plates, plasticware and napkins. There was a huge pot where the fish were frying and a grill where the hot dogs and hamburgers were grilling. People would usually order a couple of drinks before heading out back. Once they filled their bellies, they would return to the inside of the club to continue drinking and partying. I was minding my business when Luke walked up to the bar, took a seat and said, "L said you wanted to talk to me."

I'm sure I looked like a deer in headlights. I was pissed, nervous, and excited all at the same time. We conversed for a bit, and after the bar closed, he ended up going home with me.

After a whirlwind of a blessed night full of conversation and getting to know one another, amongst other things, we woke early the next morning so Luke could hit the road. Although he was from Greensboro, he was living in Rocky Mount, North Carolina with his cousin at the time and had to get back home. We vowed we were going to continue to communicate. We phoned each other every evening and spoke into the night. He was all I thought about. It felt great.

One evening, before saying our goodbyes, Luke asked if I could call him in the morning.

"Of course," I said.

"Now, don't forget."

"I won't."

The next morning, I phoned Luke. His cousin answered the phone and sounded very suspicious—odd even—when I asked to speak to Luke. "He's not here at the moment."

"But he told me to call him this morning."

"Well, he's not here. I will tell him you called though when I see him."

"Okay," I said with a confused annoyance in my voice. "Are you sure he's not there?"

"I'm sure."

"Okay, have a good day."

"You too." I hung up the phone. My instincts told me something wasn't right.

A few hours later my phone rang. I looked at the caller ID on my blue Bellsouth phone and read "Greensboro, North Carolina."

I didn't recognize the number but answered anyway.

"Hey baby, how are you? My cousin told me you called," he said.

"Luke?"

"Yeah. Hey, what's up?"

"Nothing much. I called you like you told me to and your cousin said that you weren't there. He sounded kind of funny."

"I don't know why he said that. I'm sorry. I'm here."

"Here where? Where are you?"

"In Rocky Mount."

"In Rocky Mount? No, you're not."

"Yes, I am."

"No, you're not!"

"Yes, I am!"

"If you're in Rocky Mount then how are you calling me from a 336-area code!?" Silence followed.

"Okay, I'm not in Rocky Mount."

"Then where are you?"

"I'm in jail, Cora. I'm in the Guilford County Jail," he said.

"Jail! For what!?"

"Murder."

"Murder!?"

"I'm in jail for first degree murder."

As he began to explain, I realized the murder he was locked up for, and which he would be acquitted of nine months later, was the murder of my former neighbor Angel. Luke was the tall guy running up the street. I couldn't believe it. I was stunned. After he finished explaining, we sat in silence for a while.

"I'm pregnant, Luke," I said.

We had only been courting for two weeks when I took a home pregnancy test due to experiencing extremely sore breasts and excessive sleepiness.

"It's not mine," he replied.

"You're the first person that I have been with in over two years Luke."

"Well, it's not mine," he repeated.

In the blink of an eye, my whole world had crashed. This person who I thought the world of and who I thought felt the same about me was denying that he was the father of my child. My journey of single motherhood began at that moment. Our daughter's pregnancy would be confirmed three days later at the Guilford County Health Department.

In the days that followed I became depressed. I was lying on my couch one day when I received an anonymous phone call. The caller was asking if Luke was the father of my child and if I knew anything about what had happened. He expressed to me that people were mad that Luke had something to do with the murder. I told him I didn't know Luke at the time of the incident, and I didn't know anything about what had happened.

"Well, you better watch your back," the caller said, and then hung up. I was shaken after that phone call. I was alone and pregnant with no family in the city outside of my sorority sisters.

Days after that call, one night, I received a knock at my door. "Who is it," I asked. There was no response. This scared me but I asked again, "Who is it?" Again, no response. I hesitantly looked through the peephole and saw a man standing there. My apartment was on the first floor so anything could happen, and anyone could get in if they truly wanted to. While I was looking through the peephole, the man turned and looked through it also. It was as though he was looking right at me! Was it a coincidence? Was he just peeping back to be nosey like most people did with peepholes back in the day? I don't know but I was terrified. I called the police. Normally I wouldn't, but this time I did. I feared for my and my baby's life.

The police arrived and assessed the situation. It turned out that the man had the wrong apartment. He was looking for the young lady who lived above me; they were supposed to be going out on a date that night. I didn't know. I wish I did because I would have directed him to the correct address. I surely wouldn't have phoned the police. I guess calling the police to my apartment was strike two.

Now, fast forward to the leasing office. I walked out feeling numb that day. Unbeknownst to the leasing agent, I didn't even have a job. While I was lying in my hospital bed waiting to give birth to Phoenix, L had called. He stated that I would no longer have a job because I was having a baby and that would hinder my ability to maintain my work schedule. I couldn't believe my ears. He was like a big brother to me. It hurt that he would do that, especially knowing that I had no other source of income. He was supposed to be a friend of Luke's also. Someone who said that they raised him up in the streets. I met Luke in his establishment, for Pete's sake. He's the reason why Luke was even at our daughter's birth. How could he do that to our daughter?

What was I going to do? I had nowhere to go and no income. I would be homeless within a month.

PART 2: HOMELESS

CHAPTER 3

After my lease expired, the property manager was true to her word. My lease was not renewed, and I was officially homeless. I had no money and no job. All I had was our clothes, some essentials, toys for Phoenix, and my red 1998 Pontiac Sunfire, which was paid for thanks to my mom. My furniture went into storage.

I stayed with my friend Quiana for a while, but she had three young children of her own. Phoenix and I were an extra burden, and I understood that. I eventually left Greensboro and moved back home to Fayetteville to my parent's house for a while. During that time, I helped to care for my grandmother who was sick. I also became debt free as I paid off all my debts, except for student loans, with a part-time bartending job that I had obtained. The concept of being debt free would become the greatest lesson that I learned on my journey, but one that would not be fully appreciated, applied and practiced until approximately twenty years later.

After leaving my parent's house, Phoenix and I moved back to Greensboro to my sister's house where she lived with her boyfriend and his best friend Timmie, who would eventually become my boyfriend. Timmie was a good, solid guy who cared about my daughter and me.

For example, on Phoenix's first birthday, he insisted on baking and decorating her first birthday cake. He ended up baking two cakes and decorated them with brown and white icing. He carved happy birthday messages in both—an activity he took great pride in. It made him happy. Phoenix enjoyed her cakes and her first birthday as much as a one-year-old could! It was a great day.

Shortly after Phoenix's first birthday, my mother called me one day, crying, and stated that her mother, my grandmother who had continued to live with her after Phoenix and I left, had died, and she was taking her back home to Tucson, Arizona to be buried. I immediately ran across the hall to my sister's room and gave her the phone. I went back to the bedroom that I shared with Timmie and Phoenix and sat down on the couch, thinking about how grateful I was for the opportunity to take care of my grandmother in her last days when I had previously moved back home. I also thought about how grateful I was that she and Phoenix had gotten a chance to meet each other and spend valuable time together before her passing.

After hanging up with my mother, my sister walked across the hall and entered our room, saying simply, "We have to go."

In record time my sister had booked a van, and we were packed and headed to High Point to retrieve my older brother who had recently moved there. Once he and his bag were in the van, we hit the road to Tucson, a 3,000-plus mile trip. My mom had no idea her children were on their way.

After about thirty-six continuous hours of travel, only stopping to get food, use the restroom and switch drivers, we pulled into the front yard of my aunt Betty and uncle Big Boy's house in Tucson. We all looked out the windows and could see that everyone standing in the front yard was confused and wondering who was in the big white van. We opened the driver side and passenger doors of the van and slid the side door open. At that moment, upon exiting the van, my mom realized that it was her children. That we had made the cross-country trip to be there for her and to support her. The look on her face was something that money couldn't buy, nor could it be duplicated; it was priceless. We ran and hugged her. My stepfather was standing next to her, having made the trip as well, arriving shortly after my mom once he received approval from the military.

Our extended family members were shocked yet pleased to see us as well. In return I was equally as happy to see them. I had not seen our family in Tucson and other extended family members since I was eight years old. Some I hadn't seen since I was younger than that. I was now twenty-five. It also marked the first time Phoenix was introduced to her extended family members who hailed from Texas and back west to California.

After reuniting with family and burying my grandmother, we headed home. During the trip, I couldn't help but constantly think that here I am going back to this same old bullshit. I couldn't find a job no matter how hard I tried, and God knows I was trying—hard! I didn't understand it. Why was I unable to find a job?

CHAPTER 4

Shortly after losing my apartment, I had left Greensboro and moved back home to Fayetteville with my parents for a while. Therefore, the charges that I had received the night that Zora phoned the EMS and police department to my apartment were transferred from Guilford County to Cumberland County. After attending my scheduled court dates, the consequence for the charges were having to take a drug class and earn the certificate of completion for the class which would be submitted to the court for dismissal of the charge. The instructor of the class was responsible for submitting the certificates to the court and providing each participant with a copy. After completing the course, I received mine.

Timmie, Phoenix and I were driving around Greensboro one day. While driving, I was discussing with Timmie the frustration I felt with my inability to get a job and how I couldn't understand why that was. My sister was starting to get fed up with Timmie and I being unemployed, and it looked as though we were lazy and living off her rent and bill free when the reality of it was, I just couldn't find a job for some reason. Neither could he.

As we were driving, I decided to go to my lawyer's office. I had retained a lawyer after I received my charges. Zora helped pay for it. It turned out I had picked a good time to visit with him, because he was available as soon as I walked in. After exchanging greetings, I blurted out, "I can't find a job to save my life!"

To my astonishment, he said he had been looking for me and that there was a warrant out for my arrest.

"ARREST? Arrest for what?" I asked.

He said that I was supposed to have finished my drug class, and since I didn't, there was a warrant out for my arrest!

"I completed my class a long time ago," I said. He asked if I had the certificate and I affirmed. I went out to my car in the parking lot and retrieved my certificate and accompanying paperwork from the glove compartment and gave it to him.

"Okay, good," he said. "Now go home and don't go anywhere for the rest of the day. I will call you tomorrow. I'm going to go to court in the morning to get this dismissed for you".

He phoned the next day and congratulated me as both of my charges had been dismissed. He also explained that apparently there was a failure in communication between Cumberland County and Guilford County when I moved back to Greensboro from my parent's home. Guilford County did not receive communication that I had completed my course and received my certificate and therefore had issued a warrant for my arrest. Each time I applied for a job and the criminal background was run it showed that I had a warrant for my arrest. This would be the reason why I was either never called back for a job or I was denied the position altogether.

After my legal situation was rectified, I resumed applying for jobs. Timmie was eagerly seeking employment as well. My sister was still increasingly becoming fed up with our lack of employment and feeling like she was the only one working. I believe the fact that her boyfriend, JP, had opted to stay in Phoenix as opposed to returning to Greensboro contributed to her anger as well.

See, when we went to Tucson to bury my grandmother, we learned that JP had an aunt who lived in Phoenix. She had contacted JP and told him she needed help with packing and moving out of her current apartment. I, my sister, Timmie and JP drove ninety minutes north to Phoenix from Tucson to help. Phoenix stayed in Tucson with my mom and stepdad. After we were done helping his aunt pack and move, JP made the announcement that he was going to stay with his aunt in Phoenix. We were all shocked. An argument ensued between my sister and JP. Timmie tried to convince JP to come back to Tucson with us, but he wouldn't budge. My sister was upset and hurt and there was nothing I could do about it. We all got in the car and drove back to Tucson without JP.

CHAPTER 5

Timmie and I were told by my sister that we had to go. She cited our unemployment as the reason. I was heartbroken. I couldn't understand how she could put her niece out on the street after she had just had her first birthday! I was trying hard to find employment and so was Timmie. Where were we going to go? We literally had nowhere else to go. You can't fight with someone about staying in their home, however. We had no choice but to leave. We packed up our belongings, loaded them into the Pontiac and left. I was so angry.

We ended up driving around aimlessly with nowhere to go. We would eventually end up staying the night with my sorority sister Melissa. After that, we spent some nights at Timmie's father's house, but that was just to rest. This man was old school. We could only go to his house after he got off work, which was late in the evenings, because he allowed no one in his home when he wasn't there. When he got up to get ready for work, everyone got up. When he left the house at five in the morning, everyone left the house at five in the morning. He could care less about the fact that we had a baby with us. We had to go! We would end up driving around Greensboro watching the sun come up and stopping to see friends once the day got started. It was about the only time I was happy because I felt normal.

Homelessness can break a person. It almost seems to change one's DNA, one's inner spirit, one's core! There's a time when night falls that the outside becomes lonely and cold, and the spirit grows weary. Day in and day out this can begin to break a person down. Now, whether it breaks you down and builds you back up or just breaks you down solely depends on the individual. I felt myself breaking down. Becoming someone I had never been, a constantly angry human being. My faith in God and prayer would help though. It also helped when we both landed a job.

Timmie and I received a job at an establishment that had three tiers that consisted of a sports bar, a club, and a restaurant in Raleigh. We would drive back and forth from Fayetteville to Raleigh as by this time I was tired of having nowhere to go and eventually ended up back in Fayetteville at my parent's home. One morning my stepdad and I got into an argument because he did not want Timmie living with us at the house because we weren't married. During the argument, Timmie ended up walking out of the house. He was not from Fayetteville, so I had no idea where he went. He was gone all day.

Later that evening I walked outside and found him sitting in the driveway behind my mother's car. I asked if he was okay. He said yes. He proceeded to tell me that he had spent most of the day walking, and while doing so, he had met a couple that he wanted me to meet. He said they were Five Percenters. I had no idea what that was or meant, but I trusted Timmie, so we drove to their house so I could meet them.

The couple turned out to be very nice people. They were a little older than us and had two young children that were slightly older than Phoenix. After meeting with them and explaining our situation, they agreed to let us stay with them for a while. They also agreed to watch Phoenix while we traveled to Raleigh for work in exchange for putting groceries in the house. God knows that I had never prayed harder in my life than I did when we were living with this couple. Not because they gave the slightest inkling, clue or disposition that they would harm Phoenix, or even myself or Timmie for that matter, but because one can never be ignorant to the possibility.

I must say however, my faith never wavered, and God stood like an oak. Every time we returned from work; I would look Phoenix over from head to toe. I paid attention to her demeanor, her attitude, her cry pattern, her appetite, her toileting habits, etc. I mean I paid attention to everything. I was ready for anything to happen, but not ready to forgive myself if it did. None of us were ever harmed, however, and Phoenix was always happily playing with the kids or watching a movie with them when we returned from work.

Then one evening, as they say, all good things must come to an end. The couple sat me and Timmie down and we were given a move out date about a week away. Nothing was wrong they explained, it was just time. We thanked them for everything that they had done for us and told them we understood. We had saved just about everything we earned, which wasn't much, and we had

Timmie's food stamp card. When the time came, we had no place to go and so the Pontiac that my mom bought me in my second year of college at UNCG once again became our home. I was thankful that Phoenix was too young to understand what was going on. I was determined to figure this thing out, though, because Phoenix did not deserve this life at all—a life of homelessness and living pillar to post. She deserved her own room and a place to call home. It was not the life I wanted for her. I wanted to provide better for her on my own, as an adult. As her mother.

CHAPTER 6

Having no address makes it difficult to keep a job. When you have nowhere to lay your head and rest, bathe, cook a meal, regroup, etc., it's difficult. As a result, Timmie and I lost our jobs. We lived off what we had and the kindness of others. Longtime family and friends would feed us, allow us to wash clothes, and get Phoenix cleaned and changed. Toys R Us was my friend because they had diapers in their female restrooms at the changing station at the time. I would take more than the one I'm sure I was supposed to take. I needed them, and I asked God for forgiveness as I wasn't raised to take what didn't belong to me.

Living out of a car is hell. The legs get cramped and tired from being in the same position constantly. Your back hurts from improper alignment due to either a sitting or lying position. It's difficult to keep a small area clean which can cause stress, anxiety and depression if you are used to living in a clean home. Being in constant proximity with the same people and having no privacy and nowhere to collect your thoughts can further add to the stress, anxiety, and depression you feel. People walking by with looks of judgment at a car that's packed with a majority of your earthly possessions and you buried in them slowly chips away at your self-worth, self-esteem, dignity and pride. Having to rely on others for food, your ability to shower, toilet and wash your clothes can create a feeling of humiliation although inwardly and outwardly you are grateful. Having to constantly move to rotate those good deeds or to deflect attention being drawn to you from being parked in one space too long can be exhausting. Hoping the car doesn't break down at any given moment is an entire other stress. Seeing your baby in that situation breaks your heart and further damages the spirit.

One day I decided that we could no longer live on the streets or in a car. I couldn't. I just wouldn't. I had heard of this nifty little thing called a title loan. Since my vehicle was paid for, I figured I would try and get money that way. That was my only asset. My only means of getting money. We walked into the CitiFinancial on Skibo Road in Fayetteville and applied for the loan. To my surprise, we got the loan, three thousand and some change. Later, I would slightly regret taking the loan, but when you're broke and homeless, three grand is like three hundred thousand. I thought, *I'll take it!*

We ended up moving back to Greensboro. We were able to apply and get approved for a two-bedroom, two-bath apartment. We moved in and I never felt relief like I did at that time. It felt so good to have a home again. A place for Phoenix to run around, a room to call her own, and a hot bath and meal every night. My baby was off the streets. Timmie and I were able to get a job at Schlotzky's Deli, thanks to my sorority sister, Morgan, who was a manager there at the time. I will forever be thankful for her. Timmie also managed to pick up a second job as a cook at a restaurant in downtown Greensboro. His father would pay us in food and gas money to take him across the border to Danville, Virginia to play the lottery, as it was not yet legal in North Carolina. The extra help from him was appreciated because with rent, a loan, and daycare for Phoenix, we were barely making it. The loan and a British Petroleum or BP gas credit card that I had applied for and received would be the start of my journey back into consumer debt.

Shortly after moving into our apartment, cracks in Timmie's and my relationship began to show. I believe that we were so busy surviving and trying to make it and keep Phoenix protected, safe, and loved, that once we were able to slow down, breathe and get some normalcy back, I started to realize that the struggle was the glue that held us together.

I realized that although I loved Timmie, I wasn't in love with him. I felt guilty about feeling this way particularly because this was someone who had gone through the trenches with me during such a pivotal time in my life. We both enjoyed a beer or alcoholic beverage on our off time, but Timmie's drinking began to escalate, which didn't help either. He could drink a bottle of E&J straight to the head. It would augment the sadness, anxiety, and depression he was already grappling with as a result of family and childhood trauma.

One night, Timmie and I got into a verbal fight that would lead to our breakup. Until this day, I don't remember what the fight was about. My most vivid recollection, however, is of us arguing while he was sitting against the wall, sweating profusely with a large steak knife in his hand after having consumed a large amount of E&J. I remember him being so angry that he began bending the blade of the knife with his thumb.

I was scared. I flung open the front door of our apartment to go to the neighbors and use their phone to call 911. When I did, the door slammed so loudly behind me that I realized my baby was in the apartment and not in my arms. As quickly as that door shut it was opened again, and she and I ran full speed toward one another. Phoenix was in my arms.

He followed me back out of the apartment, arguing. The knife was absent. I told him to leave. "Just go!"

We ended up back in the apartment arguing, and I was desperate to get away from him. I took the cushions off my couch and chaise and threw them to the ground below as our apartment was located on the second floor. I told him that if he didn't leave, Phoenix and I were going to jump. He told me if I really wanted him to leave, he would leave. I said I did. The next day he left. That was the end of our relationship.

I experienced peace and quiet in the days that followed. I felt a sense of relief and happiness. I feel that Timmie and I were in a codependent relationship using one another to survive, and when 'survival mode' ended, so did our relationship. I took Phoenix to daycare and continued to work and take care of us. I lived life the best I could. I wanted a fresh start, though. One with just Phoenix and me in our own home void of any bad memories. When the lease expired on the apartment, we moved.

CHAPTER 7

After leaving Treybrooke Village, the apartment complex where we lived, I was able to secure another apartment for myself and Phoenix at Addison Pointe. I retrieved my furniture from storage and eventually got us settled in. The apartment was beautiful on the inside. I especially loved the window in the sunroom that sat off the living room. The way the sunshine beamed through the window early in the morning was amazing and refreshing. It was like a divine beam of hope. It was one of my favorite parts of the apartment.

My other favorite part of the apartment was Phoenix's room. Her beautiful, shiny, light-brown colored, 3-in-1 crib was centered against the great wall. It went perfectly with the slightly darker, brown colored carpet. At the foot of the crib, in the corner, was a huge blue and yellow Fisher Price slide. A plush, pony-sized riding horse that my mom had gotten for her sat on the wall across from her crib next to the closet. In the center of the room, there was plenty of space to play. It was simple but nice and she loved it. She also loved going to the pool at the apartments. Splashing in the water was her favorite. Mine was just dipping my toes in! We were having a ball in our new place, just her and me, together.

Unfortunately, I would soon be terminated from my job at Schlotzsky's Deli due to an argument I had with the franchise owner. With rent falling behind and no prospect of a job, life started to grow dismal again until God decided to throw some more grace my way. I had applied for a job with Sears Marketing in High Point. A few weeks later I would be called in for an interview.

On the day of the interview, per usual, I had no one to keep Phoenix. I was previously able to get Chinyere, a sorority sister of mine, to keep Phoenix for another interview I had, but she was unavailable that day. So was everyone else I contacted. The only other choice I had was to take my baby to the interview with me. After reconciling with this fact, I packed her baby bag, loaded us into the car, and proceeded to my interview. I prayed for mercy as I knew that taking a baby to a job interview was *not* the status quo.

I arrived at the interview with Phoenix on my hip. I was greeted by a beautiful, petite, nicely coiffed older black woman with a Colgate smile. My nerves were immediately eased. I began to explain why I had to bring Phoenix with me to the interview and to my surprise, she said she understood. She then launched into the interview which was going very well even though Phoenix began to cry profusely about mid-way through the interview. The interviewer remained very kind. She never showed a glimpse of anger or annoyance. She did, however, take notice of my increasing frustration and embarrassment.

She smiled and explained that she understood how I felt because she was once me. She too at one time had been a single mother and had to take her daughter to an interview as well. I thought to myself, *No way!*

She politely ended the interview, "Now get home and take care of that baby. She's probably tired and hungry."

"Yes ma'am."

I left the interview feeling immensely discouraged. I felt like even though the interviewer was very kind, I was not going to get the job. I strapped Phoenix in her car seat, and we headed home. She was in the back screaming and crying, I was in the front doing the same. It was a long ride home.

A few days after the interview I received a phone call from the woman who interviewed me. I had prepared myself for the negative response as I had many times before. "You're hired for the data entry department," she said. "Orientation is in a week!"

I was speechless for a moment but then thanked her emphatically. God knew I needed this job.

Orientation went very well, and subsequently, so did the job. I was getting the hang of data entry as that was my first time doing that type of work. I loved the way that I could type on the number keypad without looking at it the same way I could the alphabet keypad—a skill I picked up courtesy of the job. I made a few friends at work and life was going pretty good even though I did not like the fact that my older brother and his "baby momma" had moved in with me a few weeks earlier. The only benefit to that was that they took care of Phoenix while I worked.

One day I overheard a co-worker talking; she was saying how between work and her nursing program at Guilford Tech, she was exhausted. I thought about how my mom had encouraged me to go to nursing school to become a nurse like her when I initially went to UNCG, but I told her I wanted to make movies instead. Part of me wished I would have listened because clearly, even though I had earned a degree in Media Studies (television, film and radio), I wasn't making any movies. I didn't even know that you could go to a community college to become a nurse. *Wait, wasn't my co-worker too old to be in school?*

Oh, well, good for her, I thought. At least she was striving for a degree and a better life.

CHAPTER 8

I went to work one day, and it started as normal, but I could tell that there was an oddity in the air. Sensing that something was amiss I began listening to the chatter around me.

The facility is closing, and people are going to be laid off with a severance package, I said to myself. I had heard of being laid off before but had never experienced it. I had heard of a severance package before, but what was that really?

Oh well, I thought, let me keep working because I know this can't be happening.

The chatter continued for weeks when one day I noticed that people were being called in one by one to human resources. The chatter then became synonymous with a matter of fact, "I told you, girl!", which had become the sentiment among the gossipers.

My heart dropped; this couldn't be real. I just started this job a few months ago. Things had just gotten back on track, and I was feeling better overall. Unfortunately, my day came.

I was typing away on my computer thinking, *If I just do well, they won't call me.*

In the middle of feverishly typing, I heard my name.

"Miss Cora King, can you please report to human resources," a voice said.

I sat for a second, still, with my head down in despair. I knew what "please go to human resources" meant.

I entered the human resources office and the same kind woman who had hired me explained to me the company's impending closing, the details of my severance package, and even offered a sincere apology with some encouragement to keep striving and to not give up. Little did she know I had *already* given up. I drove home in silence, thinking, *What am I going to do next?* I didn't know.

After sulking for a few days, I tried to pick myself up and apply for more jobs. One of the jobs I applied for was a position at WGHP Fox 8 in High Point as a studio operator. Previously, I had completed a volunteer internship at TCT, Triad Christian Television Network, in Greensboro. I absolutely loved that volunteer internship. Setting up the set, striking the set, operating the cameras, operating the character generator, assisting with lighting and audio etc., skills I learned while earning my degree at UNCG, was everything to me. I knew I wanted to work on a television studio set for a living. I would rush back to my apartment to see my name roll across the credits at the end of the show, which aired about an hour after taping. I had come to enjoy reading credits after one of my professors in college had encouraged us to always "respect the credits." He said that if you enjoyed whatever it was you had just watched, those were the people [the credits] that made it possible. It was something I would later teach Phoenix. After every film, we watched until the last credit rolled.

None of the plethora of jobs that I had applied for were proving to be a success except for the position I had applied for with WGHP. They called me back for an interview. I was ecstatic. Over the moon, as they say. My broadcast news writing teacher, Brad Jones, from my Media Studies program at UNCG was an anchor there, and I respected the man immensely.

When I found myself clubbing a smidge too much nearing the end of my undergrad career, Mr. Jones pulled me to the side after class one day. He expressed his disappointment in me and told me where I stood in his class and what I needed to do on the final project in order to pass his class, which of course I needed to graduate.

He was in professor and father figure mode. I felt it. He reminded me of my stepfather. I vowed to myself that I would make him proud. In the end, I did. I graduated. I had done very well on my final project; he left a comment on the last sheet that was penned in red ink. He let me know in so many words never to shortchange myself and my ability again and to always do my best. He stated that he was proud of me and knew I could do it. He wished me luck moving forward. Lord knows I needed all the luck in the world for this upcoming interview. This was my dream job.

The interview went very well. I was ecstatic leaving the WGHP facility. For the first time in a long time, I felt genuinely happy. I felt that I may just get the job! About a week or so later, I received a phone call.

"We really enjoyed you at your interview, however, we decided to hire someone with more experience," a male voice stated.

I thanked the gentlemen and hung up the phone. I was crushed. I cried. I thought, *This is it. I can't do it anymore. I have tried. Everything I try seems to fail.*

I looked at Phoenix and thought, *She deserves better.*

A few days later, I was standing in the kitchen one evening somewhat in a daze. I looked over at the countertop where a bottle of Clorox bleach was sitting.

I thought to myself, *If I drink that, all of this will be over.* No more pain, no more rejection, no more feeling worthless and feeling like a disappointment, and most of all, no more feeling like a failed mother and a bad parent.

I phoned my mom and told her that I needed her to come and get Phoenix. She asked what was wrong.

I said that I loved my daughter, but I didn't want her to see me kill myself.

"What!" my mother said. With heavy tears and a trembling voice, I explained that I just couldn't do it anymore. That I was tired of trying and that everything I did seemed to fail. I couldn't keep living like that, and Phoenix deserved more. She deserved better than me.

My mom tried to reason with me, but I just kept begging her to come and get my baby. Next my mother said something that would change my life and set me on a different course.

"Cora, if you promise Momma that you will hang on for just one more day, I swear I will be there tomorrow to get you. Can you promise Momma that you can hang on just one more day?"

"Yes, ma'am, I promise."

"Okay, one more day," said Momma.

"I promise, one more day."

We said I love you to one another and hung up the phone. I grabbed my baby and said to myself, "One more day."

We sat on the couch. I thought about all I had been through up until that point. I thought about meeting my daughter's father in the bar that night, I thought about how we seemed to be forging the beginnings of a nice courtship. I thought about the murder, his incarceration, the threats on the phone and getting kicked out of my apartment with nowhere to go. I thought about getting kicked out of my sister's condo for what I perceived as no reason and becoming truly homeless. I thought about the pending charges that I had that had made it hard for me to get a job in the first place.

I thought about living from pillar to post and trying to survive. I thought about stealing when stealing was something I knew was wrong and asking God for forgiveness for it. I thought about Timmie and how we were each other's rocks, but how that just didn't work out. I couldn't make myself love someone, just the same way my daughter's father couldn't make himself love me. After it was found that there was not enough evidence to charge him and he left jail, he didn't look back at us. I only knew he was out of jail because L phoned me and told me and gave me his number. This is how he ended up at Phoenix's birth. Not because he had any decency about himself at the time, but because his boy told on him.

Let's face it. Timmie wasn't Luke. That's why it didn't work. I was in love with a man who wasn't in love with me. I thought about how what I thought a family was supposed to be didn't exist for me. I never dreamed I would become a single parent. Child support was a joke.

Eleven dollars and seventeen cents a week. A box of pampers cost more than that. Fifty dollars a month in child support because Luke went back to college and was a student. What a slap in the face!

I thought about how my brother had moved into my home only to end up treating me like shit. On one occasion he took my clothes out of my closet in anger and accidentally hit Phoenix in the face with the hangers. He subsequently threw them out in the breezeway of my apartment complex because I had just done the same with his clothes. I wanted him out of my home at the time and he refused to go. I was so happy when he finally did.

I thought about how I had finally found a job only to be laid off, and how I had the opportunity to work at my dream job but was passed up for not having enough experience. How do you get experience when no one wants to hire the inexperienced? I thought about how I felt like a failure at being a mom to the most beautiful little girl in the world. I thought about how I was just exhausted and defeated. Phoenix was already asleep in my arms when I dozed off.

The next morning, my mom and my stepdad, even though they were divorced by now, were at my front door.

"Momma told you she would be here, baby." I hugged my momma tight and long. She already knew. I hugged my stepdaddy. He knew too. My momma knew I had tried, she knew I was tired, she knew I needed help and she knew most importantly that I was grateful for her presence and for keeping her promise. My stepdaddy knew I was grateful he came with my momma to help me. We packed up my apartment, loaded the cars and headed back to Fayetteville.

I had never felt relief in my life like I did that day.

PART 3: JOURNEY TO NURSING

CHAPTER 9

CNA I and CNA II

Arriving back in Fayetteville in September of 2005 and moving back in with my mom after being on my own for eight years was a bittersweet blessing. I never wanted to have to move back home, but I was grateful that at the end of the day I could.

A week to the date that I moved back to my mom's home, I received a phone call. "May I speak to Cora King, please?"

"This is she," I said.

"I'm calling from WGHP."

"Yes?"

"I was calling to see if you were still interested in the studio operator position. The person we had initially hired didn't work out."

"I gave up everything I had in Greensboro and left a week ago," I blurted out in disbelief and mild anger.

"Oh, wow, okay. Are you able to move back?" he asked.

"No," I said sternly with increasing aggravation.

"Alright, well, thank you for your time."

"Thank you, sir."

I was beyond pissed. I felt like I had gone to UNCG for four years and earned a degree that I couldn't use. Clearly WGHP was not the plan God had laid out for me. It was okay, though; He whispered a different one in my momma's ear.

My mom's plan was simple: Go to nursing school.

"That way you never have to ask anyone for anything again."

My response to her plan was simple: "YES MA'AM!"

She then said, "But first, if you really want to know if nursing is for you and if you can do it, go to school to become a certified nursing assistant (CNA)." Again, my response was, "YES MA'AM!" I gave no fight because I had tried things my way and they didn't work. It was now time to listen. My mother had suggested nursing because she herself was a licensed practical nurse or LPN.

Unfortunately, Fayetteville Tech and surrounding community colleges did not have the program available, as all programs were full. I did find an open class an hour away in Raleigh. I pounced on the opportunity. I contacted the program and paid my fees. I gathered the necessary items that I needed to begin class and so started my journey to nursing.

With my program being a little more than an hour away and full-time for four days a week, I decided to phone a sorority sister who lived in the area and ask if I could stay with her for four days out of the week and I would pay her to let me do so. Zora agreed. Yes, EMS-calling Zora. My course, my supplies, and the money for "boarding" were all gratefully paid by way of my severance package that I had received from Sears.

I had applied very reluctantly for a food stamp card as my mother always taught us to not rely on the "system" but to make our own way. Phoenix and I had to eat, though. Our bellies were not my mother's responsibility; they were mine.

My severance wasn't much but it was enough to cover my program expenses. I still needed to buy food however, so the card wasn't a bad supplement. I told myself that it was being used as a hand up and not a handout, which would later become one of my mantras. I would go to the grocery store and buy the same meal for the duration of the eight-week CNA I program: a package of Johnsonville Bratwursts, Top Ramen noodles, bread, chips, and juice. I would leave the card with my mom during my absence for Phoenix.

My first day of class went great. I scored 100% on my first test. This led my teacher to ask me a question.

"Have you ever thought about becoming a registered nurse or RN?"

"No," I said. "I'm going to be an LPN, a licensed practical nurse. What is a RN?"

She explained to me what a registered nurse was and stated, "That's how I got my Jaguar." She did have a nice Jag. With that conversation, she had managed to plant the seed for my becoming an RN.

I successfully completed my program and began looking for a job. I didn't receive my first job until February of 2006 working with a woman named Becky who would later become like family to me. I got that job because of a woman named Cody, who had to go to Georgia to attend the murder trial of her son's father. I would eventually meet her at Miss Becky's house one day and we just clicked. Cody and I are still great friends to this day. She's a great woman and more importantly, one of the best mother's I know.

I began applying for LPN school while working. After our applications had been reviewed for entrance, I attended a meeting with other applicants at Fayetteville Technical Community College's Spring Lake campus location. At that meeting, I learned that I would be put on a waiting list. I was so discouraged as I thought I was a shoo-in for the program. I had a previous bachelor's degree, had completed CNA I school with flying colors and had completed the scientific prerequisites with A's that were required for entrance into the program.

Damn it! I thought.

I was wallowing in my disappointment while sitting outside on a bench after the meeting when a friend of mine whom I knew from main campus walked up. We began talking and he told me how he had gotten into the LPN program but had to forfeit his seat for personal reasons. I told him that I was just put on the waiting list and that I wished that I was in his position. I would accept his seat WITHOUT hesitation! We laughed and parted ways. On the drive home I was saddened but no feelings of defeat were present as I had felt that I was a long way from where I had been, and I felt accomplished.

I decided to sign up for CNA II school to increase my skill set by learning tracheostomy care, wound care, ostomy care, suctioning, catheterizations etc., and to hopefully find a better position with better pay. Now, don't get me wrong. I didn't mind my CNA I jobs, but I was never one to settle. I didn't mind cleaning people's homes, fixing their meals, bathing them when needed, ensuring that they were taking their medications properly, etc. It gave me joy, honestly. I did not enjoy CNA II school, however. Not like I enjoyed CNA I school. I particularly could not stand it when the teacher announced that we would have to write a paper.

Write a paper? For what? Nah, I left that back at UNCG, I thought to myself. I went home miffed.

I continued to go to class thinking, I don't know what I'm going to do when this paper is due because I do not feel like writing it.

One day after I had gotten home from class I was sitting in my room when the phone rang. I walked into my mom's room and looked at the caller ID. I noticed that it said Fayetteville Technical Community College. I answered the phone. The voice on the other end of the line was one that I was familiar with. It was the voice of the Dean of Health Sciences on Tech's main campus.

He said, "Hi Cora, I was calling to see..."

"YES!!! I'll take it," I excitedly blurted out without thinking.

He laughed and said, "I was calling to see if you were still interested in the LPN program. A seat has become available."

"Yes, I'll take it!" I blurted out again in increasing excitement.

"Wonderful," he said. He gave me the information for orientation; I thanked him and hung up the phone. After squealing and dancing for a few seconds I called my mother at work and told her the great news! She was ecstatic. We squealed together as we both had already known that nursing was for me. I never went back to CNA II class.

PART 4: BECOMING AN LPN

CHAPTER 10

My mom paid for my LPN program out of pocket. I was beyond grateful as this meant that I would not be saddled with more student loans. I already had student loans to repay from my undergrad program at UNCG. My mom and I together shared the costs for my books, supplies, and uniforms.

LPN school was an amazing experience. The program was a pilot program that was held in the evenings on the Spring Lake campus. It was "piped" in from the main campus in Fayetteville, but we had our own instructors as well. We—the students and instructors—became a family with a main goal of succeeding. Our instructors, such as Mr. Roni Paul, pushed us to be our best selves and we pushed each other to be our best selves as well. As a class we were a success which in turn made the pilot program a success. As a result, the program continued at the Spring Lake campus a few years after our graduation. Some of us still stay in touch and speak until this day. "SLC 4 LYFE" is our slogan! Many of us went on to become RNs.

During the program, however, I did experience two obstacles. I had been receiving daycare vouchers for Phoenix to attend daycare so that I could go to work and school. Her vouchers had come up for renewal so I went to social services for my renewal appointment and thought that it would be a breeze. I was mistaken. The case worker decided that he would give me a hard time. He was considering canceling my daughter's vouchers for some unknown reason. I was almost in tears. I couldn't believe it. I was doing well, and I couldn't afford the full cost of daycare. If my vouchers were taken, I would have to quit my program and that wasn't an option. I knew my grandma Eloise, a beautiful woman who was like my grandmother but not one of my biological grandmothers, would pitch in when she could, but I didn't want to burden her, although I knew she would never see keeping Phoenix as a burden.

I gathered myself and explained to him my situation. "Sir, I am currently working and am in school and doing well. I have made no grade lower than a B+ since I have been in the program. I have only been able to do this because my daughter has been able to attend daycare which she loves and is doing well in. If you take my vouchers, I will have to stop attending school. I am trying to get me and my daughter to a place where I *don't* have to come here for vouchers or food stamps anymore."

I then proceeded to hand him proof of my semester one grades as we had just finished that semester. He must've sensed the fervor in my voice. That, coupled with verification of grades and the fact that I remained respectful and professional during our meeting, is why I believe he decided to renew Phoenix's daycare vouchers. I was relieved and grateful.

The next obstacle I experienced nearly got me put out of the LPN program due to forgetfulness. I was in biology class and had just completed my quiz when a knock rang on the classroom door.

"Do you have a student named Cora King?" a woman asked the teacher.

"Yes, that's me," I responded.

"Please follow me," said the woman. I gathered my belongings and followed the woman to a nearby classroom.

When we entered the classroom, I was asked, "Is this your purse?"

"Yes, oh my goodness, thank you. I didn't realize that I had left it in my last class because my mind was on my biology quiz that I just took."

The woman looked at me and said, "Okay. Are these the contents of your purse?"

"Yes," I said, mildly confused as to the reason why they would be going through my purse, but I then figured it was for ID purposes because how else would they find me?

"So, this knife is yours too?" she asked.

"Yes," I said without hesitation.

"You will need to gather your things and immediately exit campus as you are suspended until further notice for bringing a weapon to campus."

WTF! I thought. It was for self-defense purposes, not to harm someone intentionally.

I had a pocketknife in my purse because a few days prior to the incident, a group of girls had tried to jump me at a gas station. They were unsuccessful, however, because those were the days when I was still halfcocked when angered and they figured it would be in their best interest not to proceed after our brief confrontation.

There were two guys who I noticed were pumping gas prior to the group arriving. During the incident, I glanced over and noticed they were still present. Once the group had left, they approached me. They asked me if I was okay.

"Yeah, I'm okay," I said, still pissed at what had just happened.

One said to me, "You're a gangster for real!"

The other guy said that he had seen the group when they pulled in and he noticed that guys had gotten out of the van first. "We weren't leaving in case them dudes decided they was going to jump in (the fight)," he said.

"Thank you both so much. I appreciate you." They nodded, went to their car, and left. I never saw them again, but to this day I am still grateful for them because they didn't have to look out for someone that they didn't know. As a result of that incident, however, I began carrying a pocketknife which I put in my purse.

I left campus that day feeling like my whole world had just fallen apart from my stupidity on so many levels. Lord knows I hadn't read the student handbook because getting in trouble was never an option. I knew how to go to school and complete my studies without issue. I never imagined this happening.

I went home and immediately reached out to the head instructor of my program. She told me to hold tight, and that she would get back to me in a few days. I continued my studies at home as if nothing happened. If God showed me grace again, I was going to make sure I completed the program. A couple of days later, my instructor reached out and communicated to me that I would be meeting with her and the medical director of our program the next day.

I arrived at the meeting calm, but nervous. I was about to fight for my and Phoenix's future. I believe that is what calmed me. To my surprise, the medical director of our program was a dentist by profession. He asked me to explain to him exactly what happened and to be honest with my recollection. I recounted the incident that led to my having the knife in my purse in the first place. I told him that I had genuinely forgotten that it was in my purse and that I take full responsibility for having it and that I truly was sorry that it was brought to campus. He nodded. He asked me about my background. I told him how I was a single parent who was currently living with her mother and trying to better myself and my daughter's life.

He looked up and gave me the "You go, champ!" smile.

He then went on to explain to me how all my instructors had good things to say about me and that they thought I was one of their brightest students. They all felt that I deserved a second chance and to not be dismissed from the program. My instructor smiled and nodded at his words. Inside, I had a myriad of emotions occurring. I wanted to cry. On the outside, I remained somewhat stoic, though. He then said something that shocked me. "You're a smoker, I see."

I thought, how does he know that I smoke cigarettes on occasion?

"A pack containing a few cigarettes was found in your purse," he said.

Oh, I thought to myself without revealing my surprise.

"If you promise me that you will quit smoking, then I will allow you to remain in this program."

"I just quit," I said.

He smiled, stood up, and shook my hand. "Okay."

I believed that he knew I would try my best, as we both knew that it wasn't that easy. I did try however, and I was successful, for a while.

I returned to the program and remained focused. I kept my eye on the prize: graduation. With hard work, concrete determination, and solid dedication, I successfully completed the program in July of 2007. The plan that God had whispered in my mom's ear was a success!

CHAPTER 11

After graduation and passing boards, Lord knows I was happy when the computer screen shut off early shortly after the 85th test question. I began looking for a job after I had received my license.

My first job as an LPN was at a methadone clinic. My pay was fourteen dollars per hour. That was the most money I had made at a job in my life, you couldn't tell me anything. After working for a few months, I ended up moving out of my mother's home and moving Phoenix and I into our own condominium. We were thriving and doing well.

I enjoyed my job as a dosing nurse at the methadone clinic because of my patients, my supervising physician Dr. Parker, and the other dosing nurse I worked with, Mrs. Nancy. With her, I would come to revisit a bad habit, smoking. The job could get stressful at times, and when we went out back for a break, she would whip out a cigarette and whip one out for me too. Lord, why!? I had kicked the habit, but stress can bring you back to bad habits.

One day while working, I was told to go over to our second building as we had two that were separated by a building in between that wasn't ours and ask the nurse practitioner to sign a form.

Nurse practitioner, I thought. What is that?

I had never heard of a nurse practitioner before.

I thought, this must be the other provider Dr. Parker had told me about, the one whom he shared the building with.

I had never met her. When I was hired for the position, she was out on extended leave for a family emergency. I walked over to the building, curious to meet her.

I showed up in her office and walked to her desk where she was sitting. I began looking around the office as I listened to the music playing on her radio. My eyes eventually landed on the nameplate on her desk.

"What is a nurse practitioner?" I blurted out. She smiled and explained to me what a nurse practitioner was: an advanced practice registered nurse who held either a master's or doctoral degree. She then explained that she was a family nurse practitioner.

"What is that?" I asked.

She explained that a family nurse practitioner was a nurse practitioner that specializes in primary care across the lifespan.

"Oh, is it hard?" I asked.

She responded, "Hard, yes, but doable. If you put your mind to it, you can *definitely* do it."

"Do you like it?"

"I love it."

That was all I needed to know. After that conversation, she had planted the seed that would one day grow into me becoming a family nurse practitioner.

I made the decision after that conversation that I was going to become a registered nurse. I mentioned to my supervisor, Vanessa, one day that I was going to go to RN school. We were cool, so I thought that she would be happy for me. The attitude on her face after my announcement, however, was less than favorable. I was slightly confused at her response for a second, then I shrugged and thought nothing of it. The reason for her "attitude" however, would soon reveal itself.

Vanessa had been out of the clinic for months, filling in at our sister methadone clinics that needed help. Therefore, I stepped up and began operating at the level of a supervisor. My work was noticed by patients and other coworkers.

When she was able to visit the clinic, she would become irritated when patients would say to me, "Oh, I thought you were the supervisor."

I didn't want her to feel as though she was being disrespected, so I would correct the patient, "No, Mrs. Vanessa is the supervisor for this clinic."

When she returned permanently to the clinic, I noticed that she was unusually hard on me. She would have a constant ill attitude towards me, nit-picked things I did and called me to her office for petty reasons. I didn't understand. She seemed to be the only one who had a problem with me. I particularly didn't understand because we previously had a great friendship. I thought it was because of the "supervisor" thing. One day, it became more than I could bear.

I blurted out, "What is your problem? What did I do to you?"

Her response shocked me. "I wanted to go to RN school too. I wanted to be an RN, but I can't. Between working here and going to dialysis, I can't."

I empathized with her and genuinely felt bad that she couldn't realize her dream of going to RN school, but I sure was going. "Well, I'm still going to apply," I said. "It will not interfere with my job. I can still do my job. It's going to be the evening LPN to RN-ADN bridge program at Tech."

She stormed out of her office not pleased and I was left looking like the famous Nick Young meme, confused as hell!

I eventually applied to and was accepted into the program.

PART 5: BECOMING AN RN

CHAPTER 12

RN-ADN

I entered the LPN to RN-ADN bridge program held on the main campus of Fayetteville Tech the Fall of 2008, paying for the program with my own money that I had saved from working. The program would last three semesters, one calendar year. The only thing that was similar between that program and the LPN program were some of the students. Most of the teachers didn't show the same care as the teachers in the LPN program did, and the family atmosphere was diminished. One instructor however, Mrs. Sivels, did show that she cared. She would make an impact on me that lasts until this day.

My first day of class during this program was extremely memorable. I had no pen, no paper, no books, no nothing. I was just there. I felt I didn't belong. Why I had that feeling, I didn't know. We were receiving various handouts such as syllabi, calendars, general instructions etc., when I received a call from Phoenix's daycare. She had gotten into trouble, and I was asked to come to the daycare.

I left during the middle of class, which was held in an auditorium, so the seating style consisted of tight rows that I had to continuously say, "Excuse me," to get out of. I was annoyed.

After tending to business at the daycare, I went home. I had scolded Phoenix for misbehaving and for my having to leave class as a result.

I felt bad for having scolded Phoenix and started crying. I felt embarrassed for having to leave in the middle of class on the first day. I felt that I should not even go back. Maybe I should just quit. Maybe this isn't for me right now. Maybe I'm overzealous. I wasn't even prepared. I cried harder.

I quelled my emotions and frustration with a couple of shots from a Seagram's Gin bottle that was sitting on the kitchen counter and indulged in a few tokes off a piece of blunt that was left in an ashtray. I then took a long, hard stare in the mirror and made a decision. I would not succumb and be a victim to my own negative thoughts. I would not be my own worst enemy and fall prey to my own self-doubt. I was a great nurse and deserved the opportunity to further my career.

I returned to class.

After class, my instructor came up to me and said as politely and sternly as she could, "Some students in your immediate area said they smelled marijuana. It is against school and program policy to use drugs and if you know of anyone that might be doing so, please let me know."

I nodded my head.

"Okay," she said with an even more polite smile that said, "Don't you ever come back into this school or program like you are now. Ever!"

I don't think I breathed again until I got in my car. One thing is for sure, I NEVER did that again.

Vanessa was continuing to give me a hard time at work every day. When you're a single parent, working and attending school, any amount of extra stress is a problem. One afternoon, the daily harassment had taken its toll. On my break that afternoon, I sat on the steps outside of our second building, and I phoned my mom.

"Mom, she keeps harassing me and I'm tired of it. I'm going to quit."

"Well Baby, do what you must do; don't quit school though."

"Don't worry, I won't." I hung up the phone and put in my two weeks' notice.

CHAPTER 13

I had a little money saved up that carried us for a little while, and I do mean a little while, but my mom was the real MVP! She made sure the rent and utilities were paid and that we had groceries. My baby brother Harold even chipped in six hundred dollars one month to help us out on rent. I cut the cable as it was an extra, unnecessary bill. Phoenix and I survived on two DVDs, Coach Carter and the Lion King 1 ½. We had other DVDs, but those were the main two we watched. Or mainly, she did. I was feverishly studying for a math quiz that meant the difference between being able to complete the program or not, and it was my third and final attempt.

You see, math had never been my strong suit. It was that area in school that I had to work extra hard on to make good grades. Nursing school would prove to be no different. I had already taken the exam twice. After the first exam, students were promised that they would receive remediation if they did not pass the exam. However, the remediation that was set in place for students never happened. We ended up examining again and I failed the second test as well.

After the test, one of the instructors pulled me into her office and stated, "I'm sorry, but you always have the opportunity to apply and come back next year and finish out the program."

"Next year!?" I began protesting the fact that we as students never received the remediation that we were promised. With remediation, it was possible that I could have made a passing grade on the exam.

"I'm sorry, Miss King, but there's nothing I can do." *I have heard that before.* I thought.

I walked out of her office once again feeling dumbfounded and defeated, but not upset, because I knew I had tried my best!

As I was passing Mrs. Sivels office, I heard, "Miss King, step into my office please."

I stepped into her office and plopped down in the seat next to her desk.

"I don't care what she says, you're right. You all did not get the remediation that you were promised. Here's what I want you to do." She gave me the information to a place on campus where I was to go in and explain that I was there to receive remediation for a medication exam in the ADN program. She then gave me a book entitled *Math for Meds*. "Here, take this. Use this at home and in conjunction with your on-campus remediation. Keep coming to class and I will get back with you. You just make sure you do what I ask you to do."

"Yes ma'am."

I immediately left her office and went right over to speak to someone about remediation. A few days later after class, Mrs. Sivels came to me and said, "You are allowed one more attempt at the exam. This is your last and final attempt."

"Yes ma'am, I understand."

Every day, night and weekend, almost around the clock for two weeks, I ate, slept, and breathed math. I only stopped for bathing, cooking, cleaning and taking care of Phoenix. Occasionally I would study my other materials, but math was my priority.

The day of the exam I was calm, yet nervous. I knew Phoenix and my future depended upon me passing this test. I couldn't fail. I wouldn't fail. I thought I had put in work studying for the second test, but you don't know what putting in work is until you know your baby girl's livelihood depends on your success and not your failure and you alone are responsible for it.

Mrs. Sivels proctored my exam. It was just me and her in an empty classroom. She handed me my exam.

"Good luck." She went and sat at a desk to the side of and behind me, opened her novel, and began reading. I turned around, prayed, and began the exam.

Everything looked foreign because of my anxiety. I second guessed everything I did. Lord knows I was sweating. Phoenix was heavy on my mind. I prayed, calmed myself and refocused.

After what seemed like the longest sixty minutes of my life, I finally said, "Done."

I handed over my exam like I was handing over the keys to my newly purchased Aston Martin to a reckless teenager with no license and a penchant for trouble. I was shaking in my boots! After melting in my seat during grading, which felt like an eternity, Mrs.

Sivels turned to me with a brief stoic look. My heart dropped. "You passed."

"I passed?"

"You passed!"

"I passed!" I screamed. "We did it, Phoenix!" We were going to be just fine. I knew we were I had no doubt about it.

I finished out the rest of the semester, then it was time for finals. After completing our final exam, we waited out in the hallway to be called in the office for our final grades. Most of us rejoiced as we found out that we had passed our exam. One student who found out they did not pass their exam was one of my best friends, Tina. The same teacher who took no issue with saying that I could apply next year for the program was the same teacher who took pleasure in telling Tina, in front of a hallway full of people, that she didn't pass the exam. And if you're thinking, *Hallway? I thought you said you were called into the office.*

If you thought that, you are correct. The courtesy was not given by this teacher to call Tina into her office. Her goal was to embarrass Tina, and we knew it. That's how some of the teachers in the program were.

Upon overhearing this news, the rejoicing ceased. Disbelief and anger followed.

"You didn't have to call her out like that," one person said to the instructor.

"You could have privately called her to your office," I said to the instructor.

Tina looked hurt but resilient. I quickly turned to my friend and said, "I don't care what that instructor says. You are smart, you are strong, and you are one of the best nurses I know. Next year you come back stronger and better, and you pass this program and never look back."

"Oh, I will, don't you worry," Tina said. That is exactly what she did as she graduated the following year!

CHAPTER 14

RN to BSN

My first job out of RN school was at Cape Fear Valley Medical Center, the biggest hospital in Fayetteville, North Carolina. I began work there as a licensed registered nurse in August of 2009. I worked Med/Surg telemetry on three south. It was there that I became a skilled floor nurse. I honed my skills under the tutelage of LPNs who were amazing and very skilled nurses. They possessed as great or greater skill than some RNs. They knew the meat and potatoes of nursing as some had been practicing for twenty plus years. I realized then that a nurse with a higher degree didn't necessarily mean that they were a "better" nurse as some would like to believe, it just meant that they took a different educational path to their nursing career. My next path would be a BSN program.

I had to take a math class prior to enrolling in the BSN program at Fayetteville State University, which was held on that same campus. It was a semester long. I was in no hurry, though; one class was a nice break from the usual full-time schedule I usually maintained. I completed the course and the following semester enrolled full-time in the online RN-BSN program. It would take one calendar year to complete.

"No problem," I said to myself, "I have done this before."

I had made it through the first semester, and the second semester was going very well. But, as I said before, it is extremely tough to be a single, full-time working parent. Life stepped in and I had to step out of the program, leaving in the middle of a semester. I contacted my program and let them know that I would be withdrawing so that I could receive an "I" for incomplete as opposed to an F. With that, I had the option to return to the program in the courses I left. It would be Tina that would get me back on my game, and I wouldn't stop until I became Dr. King, Family Nurse Practitioner, Board Certified.

Sitting in my room one day with my dialysis scrubs on, having just walked home from work to save on gas as my job was across the street from my neighborhood, I received a phone call.

"King, what's up?" said a familiar voice on the other end of the phone.

It was Tina. We hadn't spoken in a while.

"Oh, nothing much, sis, what you up to?" I responded.

"Nothing much sis. So, I enrolled in the program at Fayetteville State to get my BSN and I need help with this class."

"Oh, sis, I'm sorry, I can't help you there. That is the exact class that I left the program in. I had to quit, but I am so proud of you."

"Quit?" said Tina in bewilderment.

"Yeah." I retorted.

"Wait a minute. You don't quit nothing. You are one of the smartest people I know," said Tina.

"I had to quit sis."

"King..." said Tina as she began to give me the third degree about exiting the program.

After we ended our conversation and hung up the phone, I had literally, without exaggeration, took the money I had managed to save in my savings account, approximately $1,700 dollars, and paid it out to Fayetteville State University. Yes, I had re-enrolled in school thanks to Tina and her motivational sermon. Sometimes you just need that one nonjudgmental person who gives a damn about you when you need it. I was grateful for my friend.

Tina and I vowed that we would finish our BSN degree and cross that stage together. We were we each other's champion, each other's rock. Our support for one another never wavered, not even when I moved to Atlanta without Phoenix for a brief four months, as I had transferred my dialysis job there. My intention was to start a life for Phoenix and me there and send for her once I got established. That never happened. My mom phoned me one day and said that Phoenix was not faring well with me being gone. I left Atlanta in December 2012.

Upon my return to Fayetteville, Tina and I didn't skip a beat. We made it all the way through the program and finished up with our required capstone projects. My capstone project, entitled 'Preventing the Spread of Disease: Infection Control in School-Age Children,' would proudly be executed in Phoenix's fourth grade classroom. She was so proud of me being her momma, and I was so proud to be her momma. We were advancing together like always and it felt great to be able to include her physically in my educational journey for the betterment of our lives.

I remained unemployed for a short period of time before finding employment in a nursing home after returning to Fayetteville. While unemployed, graduation time had rolled around and I essentially had no money. I almost didn't make it to our department pinning ceremony- a ceremony that students' families are invited to that welcomes those nurses that are new to the profession and symbolizes completion of the program for everyone. We were to bring our own pins to be pinned with. I couldn't find mine, let alone something to wear, and was mildly depressed as a result, although I would not let it be known.

Tina and I were on the phone one day and the conversation of going to the ceremony was the topic. Tina insisted that I attend and not to worry about being pinned, as I had expressed that concern to her. She can be a very persuasive individual who loves hard and with all her heart. So, at the end of another of her motivational sermons, I agreed to attend the pinning ceremony.

Tina brought two pins with her to the ceremony. The BSN pin that was for purchase prior to our pinning ceremony and her RN pin she received during our ADN program. We were lined up to enter onto the stage for pinning and to receive our degree case. Like a comedic film scene, Tina and I were quietly arguing back and forth about who's going to get pinned with what pin as we stood in line on the side of the stage.

"I am not getting pinned with your BSN pin. I'll take the RN pin," I said.

"No, you are getting pinned with the BSN pin. I don't care what you say."

"No!" I responded.

"Cora!"

"No, you take it," I said.

People in the audience started to take notice of our communication, to which we would glance over and smile sweetly and then resume the back and forth.

When my last name was called, which was alphabetically before Tina's, she forcefully placed the BSN pin in my hand and gently shoved me up the last step and onto the stage. I turned around annoyed, but was met with a large smile spread across Tina's face. I turned back around, was pinned, politely shook the presenter's hand, received my degree case and exited the stage. Tina would soon follow. Later we would laugh about the occasion. We attended the main university graduation a few days later and we had officially met our goal, we were registered nurses with a Bachelor of Science in Nursing degree! We now had the ability to pursue a graduate nursing degree. I was ready to make good on my long time promise to myself, my dream of becoming a nurse practitioner. I began my research of programs very shortly after graduation.

PART 6: BECOMING AN FNP

CHAPTER 15

Researching family nurse practitioner programs was a task that I took great pleasure in. I was determined not only to find a good program to attend but one that would not cause me any further student loan debt. I had student loans from my 2001 undergraduate degree from UNCG and did not care to further go into educational debt. For schools, I narrowed my search down to two. The University of North Carolina at Wilmington (UNCW) and East Carolina University (ECU). UNCW offered a two-year Master of Science in Nursing degree program with a family nurse practitioner concentration. In contrast, ECU offered a three-year Doctor of Nursing Practice degree program with a family nurse practitioner concentration. I intended on applying to both universities after I completed my testing and received results for the Graduate Record Examination or GRE.

I prepared for the GRE by buying a study book from Barnes and Noble. I began studying, focusing mainly on math, because as we all know, that's my area of struggle. My second focus was preparing for the written portion. English was always my strong suit in school but having to write concisely and effectively under time constraints was where I needed practice. I rounded out my studying with the vocabulary portion. After a few months of consistent, weekly study, I registered to take the GRE examination in Raleigh.

I booked a hotel room so that I could travel to Raleigh the day before the exam. The goal was to be relaxed prior to the exam and to not have to worry about anything adverse happening on test day. I was not giving Murphy's Law any leeway if I could help it. Phoenix, myself, and my friend Diamond traveled to Raleigh the day before the exam. We hung out in the hotel room, mainly enjoying the fact that we were out of Fayetteville.

The morning of the exam, I was all nerves. I tried to quell them to the best of my ability. I showered, ate breakfast, and headed to the testing site. I began the test without issue, but about halfway through, I got "the bubble guts," my stomach started to turn due to my nerves and I requested a bathroom break. Upon my return, I ignored the fact that I had let time lapse that I couldn't get back and instead focused on doing the best I could on the remainder of the exam. When it was over, I was relieved. I would later come to find out two things after testing.

First, I did well enough on my GRE that I could now officially apply to graduate school. Second, I learned that the GRE would be suspended for five years, starting the following year, related to the theory that the examination was not indicative of one's success in graduate school.

Really? Go figure, I thought, miffed that that conclusion was not drawn a year or two sooner. If that had happened, it would have saved me a lot of stress and money.

CHAPTER 16

I had gathered all my necessary documentation and applied to both universities. I eagerly awaited their responses. UNCW was the first school to respond with a letter of declination. I was devastated. I thought that if a master's program turned me down, there was no way a doctoral program was going to accept me. What was I going to do? I had only applied to two schools and had planned my life out accordingly. A plan that spanned the next two to three years dependent upon what program accepted me. I figured that if I didn't make it, I would have to go back to the drawing board and formulate a new plan, but I vowed that I would not give up. One day the letters FNP would be behind my name and the opportunity for a better position and salary would be ahead of me.

As I was walking out of the Dollar General one afternoon and heading into the Food Lion, I got an email alert on my phone. It was an email from ECU. I opened the email and the first word I read was, "Congratulations."

Tears started to stream down my face as I knew what congratulations meant. I continued reading. My acceptance was contingent upon how well I did during my first semester of school.

I thought to myself, don't you worry, you won't be disappointed for accepting me into your university.

I called my mom to share the news. We rejoiced and hung up. I dried my eyes and proceeded into Food Lion.

A major task I completed while applying to school was securing a way to pay for school. After much research, I came across federal educational loans for service (FELS) on the North Carolina State Education Assistance Authority (NCSEAA) website. FELS seemed to be a little too good to be true, so I phoned the NCSEAA. The person on the phone explained that FELS was funded through money that the North Carolina General Assembly held in their education fund. If there was enough money in the "pot," monies would be distributed directly to the school listed on the applicant's application.

For the program I was enrolling in, a doctoral program, the FELS would pay $14,000 a year, $7,000 a semester, excluding the summer, directly to the school on my behalf. Any residual monies would be refunded to the student per the school.

In order to repay the loans, you had two options: either pay the loan back in cash or through your service. This meant that you had to either work full-time anywhere in the state of North Carolina for one year or part-time anywhere in the state of North Carolina for two years to pay back one year of the loan.

I thought, I can do that.

I don't mind working off my debt as I would rather work and make money while paying back a debt than pay cash for the debt. If you wanted to renew the loan and continue receiving the money the following year, you only needed to reapply, which was as simple as clicking a button stating you wished to renew the application if none of your information had changed. I would find this out in subsequent years.

I filled out the application and was approved for the loan. The monies were distributed to the university as stated. In addition to this, grant monies awarded to the ECU graduate school of nursing were divided and distributed to each student's account.

I worked as a dialysis nurse during the program, working every Friday and Saturday. I worked more during breaks and between semesters. This was because I had enrolled in the program full-time which stated you could only work so many hours a week as the program was rigorous. These three sources of finance were how I paid for school and ran my household during my time at ECU.

CHAPTER 17

Orientation was held on campus in Greenville, NC and I knew that first day I was where God wanted me to be and that I would be successful there. I also met a person with whom I formed a great bond of sisterhood and who would be my rock during this journey. She was one of my champions and I hers. We were two of only a handful of black students in the program. She was a fellow classmate named Tikia. We hit it off immediately. I believe that we shared an unspoken understanding of and appreciation for what led to our meeting and how important it was, as women of color, to finish the program successfully.

The program would indeed prove to be an extremely rigorous one. The program was didactic, meaning that it was online with campus meetings every semester that spanned the length of four to five days. These were some of my favorite times during the program as I found that we all needed one another. There was a lot of excitement in seeing who you were in the "struggle" with. We exchanged phone numbers and added one another to Facebook. This exchange didn't initially happen at orientation, I feel, because we were all in the "zone" and trying to absorb all the information we were being inundated with. Also, obviously, we didn't know each other. As a result of the exchange, however, some of us would end up keeping in constant contact throughout the program, serving as a continuous support system for one another.

I was matriculating through the program successfully, through all the assignments, discussion boards, endless papers, group projects, clinicals, etc., when my resilience and ability to persevere would once again be tested. I was in the third year of the program and was already extremely stressed and having trouble as this was the year that development and construction of our final DNP scholarly projects began. Concurrent with this, I had been experiencing increasing difficulty with Phoenix, so much so that I would end up having to start the development and construction of my final project over, which put me behind and unable to graduate with my class.

I needed advice on what to do with Phoenix's negative behavior. One day at the end of March, I went to the director of my program, Dr. Skipper, and asked if I could speak with her. She was a sweet woman who was very approachable and easy to talk to. I began to tell her that I was having a hard time with Phoenix and that she was continuously getting into trouble.

After listening to my concerns, she looked me square in the eye and with her motherly eye, finger and tone said, "You better put her on birth control, and you better put her on birth control now. As soon as you get home. If she is displaying that type of behavior and participating in those types of things, then she's more than likely going to try sex if she hasn't already. I've seen it many times before." She then concluded with a stern, "As soon as you get home."

"Yes, ma'am. Thank you."

I turned around and thought to myself, I am so busy and so strapped for time, not to mention exhausted from my current schedule. I will take her as soon as the semester ends in May."

Besides, she was only 14 and we had had conversations about sex and protection, about STIs and HIV. I thought to myself, *I didn't raise her like that. My baby wouldn't do that.*

CHAPTER 18

I was partaking in my annual spring cleaning one afternoon as I had decided to take a break from studying. It was a beautiful sunny day, and Phoenix was out hanging with her friends. I had my music playing, and I was in the groove when I heard a knock at the front door. It was Phoenix and two people that I knew, one whom I considered my best friend at the time and hung out with regularly when I wasn't in school and whom Phoenix called "Auntie." The other was my best friend's friend who was an acquaintance of mine as well.

I let them in, not noticing the look of seriousness on their faces as the glare of the sun beaming through the front door blinded me, and returned to my cleaning duties in one of the bedrooms. "Aye, you all want to help? I could use it," I said smiling. I heard no response.

"We need to talk," I heard the acquaintance say in a very serious voice. I came out of the room, confused and mildly concerned at her tone, and walked into the dining room.

Phoenix was sitting at the dining room table looking down at the floor.

"What? What's up? What's going on? Phoenix, why are they looking like that?"

"Phoenix has something she wants to tell you," said the acquaintance.

"Tell me what, Phoenix? What's up? What's going on?" I said with increasing concern. She then looked up at me with sadness and fear in her face, not uttering a word.

Impatient, the acquaintance then blurted out, "Phoenix is pregnant."

After standing stunned and in disbelief for a moment, I responded, "No she's not."

"Yes, she is," said the acquaintance.

I looked at Phoenix and with a mild laugh, as I thought this was all a joke and stated, "No you're not. You know better. You're not even having sex. You're only fourteen."

"Yes, she is," said the acquaintance again.

I looked around at everyone, confused, and then I heard, "Mommy, yes, I am. I'm pregnant."

I immediately dropped to my knees in tears, asking God why. *I can't take much more; this can't be happening.*

I stood up, gave my best friend my credit card and had her go to the Dollar General to buy a pregnancy test. She returned shortly thereafter, and Phoenix took the test. Result positive.

My life forever changed that day. My daughter was two months shy of her fifteenth birthday and pregnant.

I thought, what if I would have just listened to Dr. Skipper just a few weeks earlier in March? How different things would be.

I didn't though. And now, here we were. Me and my acquaintance were going to be teenage grandparents as her son was the father. This was the reason for the serious voice, and this was the reason she felt compelled to blurt out that Phoenix was pregnant.

I would only be taking one class during the summer and fall semesters as I had finished all my regular program requirements except for my final DNP scholarly project. This allowed me to be able to quit my job at the dialysis center and sign up as a travel nurse. I first travel nursed in Columbia, South Carolina. I met a lot of great people during my time there. People that allowed me to make it through such a tough time. One such person, Crystal, the front desk manager at the dialysis facility, and her husband Vincent, opened their home up to me. They allowed me to sleep in their daughter's room who was away at college. They charged me nothing. This allowed me to save on gas, lodging, and travel which in turn allowed me to save more money for my grandson. By this time, we had found out the sex.

I later asked Crystal why she and her husband did it, why they invited a stranger to stay in their home. She responded, "Because God told me to."

Words I'll never forget. I was grateful to them both. We keep in touch until this day.

My assignment after Columbia was in Greenville. I strategically chose that city so that I could be in the same town as ECU for my last semester. It worked out beautifully. I was able to stay with Tikia, who lived nearby in Winterville, thereby allowing me to continue to save as much money as I could for my grandson. Also,

I was able to visit school as much as I needed to, which was of great help when it came to me completing my DNP scholarly project.

I would present my final project entitled, "Improving HPV Vaccination in Adolescents: A Quality Improvement Initiative," an accomplishment that was made possible with the great help of my amazing project champion, Dr. Reilly, on November 8, 2018. My mom, Phoenix, my nephew Cleophas, and my friend Xavier all attended my presentation to show their support. Tikia and her cousin Lisa- also my friend- had attended the presentation as well.

My Greenville assignment ended on December 7, 2018, one week prior to my graduation. On December 8, 2018, I, along with various friends and family members, threw Phoenix a beautiful baby shower. It was wonderfully planned and executed by my baby sister Tiangela and her girlfriend at the time, Vonia, a.k.a. Tree, as she is affectionately called by family because of her height. Tree's mother, Mrs. Tausha, catered the occasion. Shontae took care of the photography. The event was enjoyed by all!

Six days later, on December 14, 2018, I graduated with a Doctor of Nursing Practice Degree with a concentration of family nurse practitioner. My graduation was attended by my mom, Phoenix, my baby brother Harold, my older brother Craig, my nephew Cleophas, his girlfriend Daysha, my sisters Denise and Tiangela, my niece Princess, my nephews Prince and Dewayne, my nephew Tim, and one of my best friends Cordell (Shaun), who managed to capture the occasion on video.

Mission, goal, and dream accomplished! Twenty-two days later, my grandson, Major, arrived in this world on January 5, 2019!

Currently my grandson is being raised by myself and my dad, his great-grandfather, who moved from Detroit, Michigan to help. He is thriving and doing very well. He often receives compliments on his manners and behavior from his teachers and other community members even though he's only three years old, but I attribute that to being 'raised from an old school' and having a positive male role model in the home.

Phoenix is currently in school and is on schedule to graduate in May of 2023 through an alternative high school program that allows students who have previously quit school to pick up where they left off. Students can complete the credits required by the state for graduation and therefore may earn their high school diploma. The school also offers multiple resources to single teenage parents such as daycare, diaper assistance, and food donations, amongst other things.

Unfortunately, there is no relationship between Phoenix and the father of her child, and Major has never met his father. His father has chosen not to be a part of his life. His paternal grandmother has seen him physically twice: once in December of 2019 and one other time shortly thereafter, in 2020. Despite these challenges and history of single motherhood repeating itself, I am grateful that I was able to thwart the poverty that sometimes comes along with being a single mother as a result of having no education, no stable career and income, no stable home, no stable transportation, and no father or other positive, strong male role model in the home.

I am grateful that I was able to provide a financially secure upbringing for my daughter and that I can now provide a financially secure upbringing for my grandson via a profession that I love. Florence Nightingale, the founder of professional nursing, stated what nursing was to her: "Service to God in the relief of man." By providing this, I have been able to achieve and experience relief for myself, my family and others.

PART 7:
IF I CAN DO IT,
SO CAN YOU!

CHAPTER 19

Across my career, I have met several women, young and old, who say proudly, "I'm a nurse!"

My first thought was always, "You just said you were a CNA."

"I am!" they would proudly proclaim.

"That's not a nurse," I would say. "A licensed and/or registered nurse does not have the term 'assistant' in their title."

Some would get angry, and some would accept what I was saying.

I thought, this person wants to be a nurse, but someone may have not told them that they could be a nurse, so they adopted their current position as such because the word 'nursing' was in the title.

As a result of this, my thought was that not only is education needed, but maybe a little inspiration and hope.

My last role as a registered nurse was as a staff development coordinator for a long-term care facility. Part of my job was to orient and educate the newly hired staff. One day, I walked into a class full of young black women and one older white woman. After introducing myself as Dr. King, family nurse practitioner non-board certified (I had not yet sat for board certification), a lot of questions ensued.

I answered as many as I could with my usual zeal and fervor.

I ended with this: Don't let anyone tell you what you can't be. Young black women are not meant to be *just* a CNA for the duration of their career in health care (a thought shared by many in the south). If that's what you want to be, then that is completely fine. There is no judgment as we *do* need CNAs in the healthcare field.

However, you *can* further your education if you want to. You can become those individuals to whom you answer to. Your superiors. The field is wide open. You can become what you want. It is possible and I am a testament to it. Remove the barriers one by one and become exactly what it is you want to be. Most importantly, remember, you control your own destiny.

The entire room began to ask questions about nursing programs. I began to speak on everything I possibly knew that could help to include ways that they could fund their education without creating student loan debt. I spoke on childcare, research, and the importance of meeting deadlines. All of it. All of what I knew. I could see their wheels spinning. They were beginning to think new thoughts. I could see the "if she can do it, so can I" look on their faces.

At the end of class that day, everyone thanked me for taking the time to speak with and educate them. The older white woman approached me and thanked me and said she learned a lot as well and felt inspired also.

"No problem," I said, "What I have to say is for everybody. No matter your background."

The next day while in the breakroom, one of my class attendees walked in. "Dr. King," she said.

"Hey, what's up?" I responded.

"I just wanted to let you know that I went to Fayetteville Tech yesterday and got some information. I am enrolling in their LPN program next fall. I just wanted to tell you thank you."

"Congratulations," I said, and gave her a big hug. "That's awesome, and no problem, it was my pleasure. Good luck here and with your future studies."

Inside, I was beaming with pride.

When you talk to someone about your journey you have no idea of the impact and inspiration it can have on them. We are all in this struggle called life. We can all use a little inspiration, a little education, and a little information. Never be afraid to pay your blessings forward. Information and sharing can be a blessing. We all have the potential and ability to positively impact the world in which we live through our own individual testimonies.

I will leave you with this, don't ever say what you can't do, no matter the circumstance. You must keep your faith as small as a mustard seed, believe in your Higher Power, whomever it may be, and believe wholly in yourself and your capabilities. Understand that your dreams and visions are God's eyesight for you.

Oprah once said, "God can dream a bigger dream for you than you can dream for yourself, so surrender."

Please surrender, because if I can do it, SO CAN YOU! May God bless us all!

THE MARATHON CONTINUES
– Nipsey Hussle

Printed in Great Britain
by Amazon

26912946R00056